# spot

## BABY FARM ANIMALS

## DUCKLINGS

by Anastasia Suen

AMICUS | AMICUS INK

foot

eye

Look for these
words and pictures
as you read.

bill

wing

Have you ever seen a duckling?

A duckling is a baby duck.
It hatches from an egg.

Look at the duckling's foot.
It has webbed toes.
A duckling swims
the day it hatches.

foot

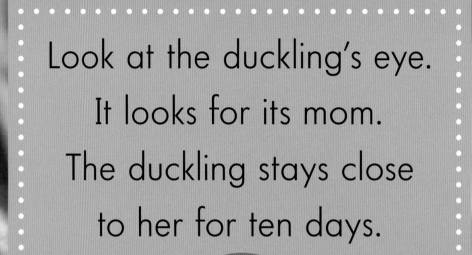

Look at the duckling's eye.
It looks for its mom.
The duckling stays close
to her for ten days.

eye

Look at the duckling's bill.

A duckling eats bugs.

A duckling eats plants, too.

bill

## wing

Look at the duckling's wing.
It will grow new feathers.
Soon the duckling will fly.

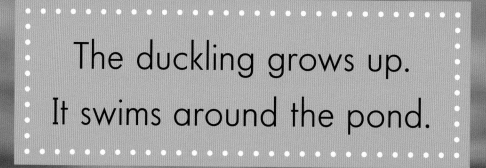

The duckling grows up.
It swims around the pond.

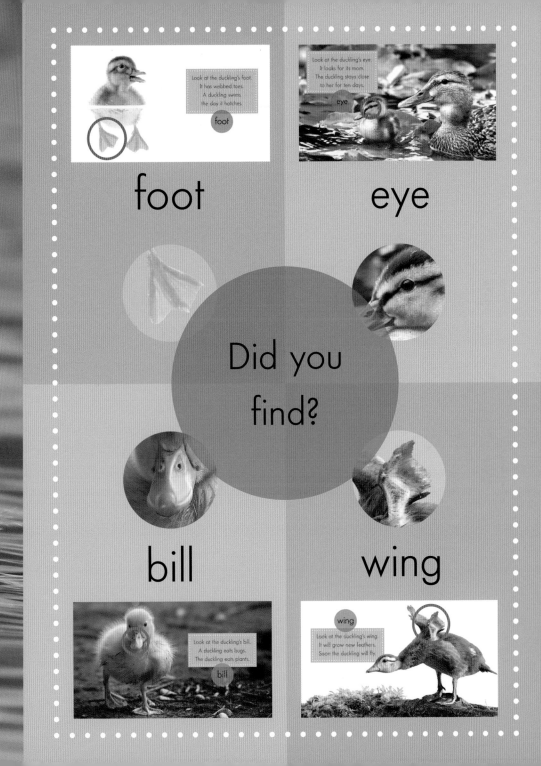

foot

eye

Did you find?

bill

wing

# spot

Spot is published by Amicus and Amicus Ink
P.O. Box 1329, Mankato, MN 56002
www.amicuspublishing.us

Library of Congress Cataloging-in-Publication Data
Names: Suen, Anastasia, author.
Title: Ducklings / by Anastasia Suen.
Description: Mankato, MN : Amicus, [2019] | Series: Spot.
 Baby farm animals
Identifiers: LCCN 2017046900 (print) | LCCN 2017049411
 (ebook) | ISBN 9781681515687 (pdf) | ISBN 9781681515304
 (library binding) | ISBN 9781681523682 (pbk.)
Subjects:  LCSH: Ducklings--Juvenile literature.
Classification: LCC SF505.3 (ebook) | LCC SF505.3 .S84 2019
 (print) | DDC 636.5/97--dc23
LC record available at https://lccn.loc.gov/2017046900

Printed in China

HC 10 9 8 7 6 5 4 3 2 1
PB  10 9 8 7 6 5 4 3 2 1

Wendy Dieker and
 Mary Ellen Klukow, editors
Deb Miner, series designer
Aubrey Harper, book designer
Holly Young, photo researcher

Photos by Shutterstock/Ohlastock
cover, DenisNata 1; iStock/
valentinrussanov 2, 6–7, 15,
Edith64 2, 10–11, 15, leekris 14;
Alamy/frans lemmens 2, 8–9, 15,
tbkmedia.de 3, Anyka 4–5; Getty/
Jim Cumming 2, 12–13, 15

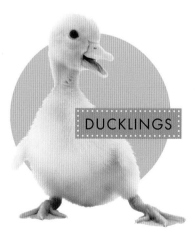

DUCKLINGS